Mantua Travel Guide 2025

An Overview of the City's Top Attractions

Vena D. Veny

Copyright©2025

Table of Contents

Introduction

Mantua, or Mantova in Italian, is a city of profound historical and cultural significance in the Lombardy region of northern Italy. Nestled in the Po Valley, Mantua is surrounded on three sides by artificial lakes created by the Mincio River, which gives the city a unique and picturesque setting. These lakes, Lago Superiore, Lago di Mezzo, and Lago Inferiore, were engineered in the 12th century to fortify the city against invaders. Today, they contribute to the city's scenic beauty and tranquil atmosphere.

With a population of approximately 47,000 residents, Mantua is a manageable size for visitors to explore and experience its rich heritage. The city's compact layout allows for easy navigation on foot or by bicycle, making it an ideal destination for leisurely exploration. Mantua's blend of architectural styles, from mediaeval fortifications to Renaissance palaces, reflects its complex history and the various powers that have ruled it over the centuries.

Mantua is not only an architectural gem but also a vibrant cultural hub. It hosts numerous festivals, concerts, and theatrical performances throughout the year. The city is particularly famous for the Festivaletteratura, an annual literary festival that attracts writers, poets, and readers from around the world. Additionally, Mantua's culinary scene is renowned for its traditional dishes, which showcase the rich agricultural produce of the surrounding countryside.

Mantua's history is a tapestry of cultural and political influences that have shaped its development over millennia. The city's origins date back to the Etruscan civilization, which settled in the area before being overtaken by the Gallic Cenomani tribe. In 220 BCE, Mantua became a Roman colony, marking the beginning of a period of prosperity and growth. The city gained prominence as the birthplace of the great Latin poet Virgil, who was born in 70 BCE in the nearby village of Andes (now Pietole).

In the mediaeval period, Mantua rose to prominence as a fief of Boniface of Canossa, marquis of Tuscany, in the 11th century. After the death of Matilda of Tuscany in 1115, the city established a communal government and became an important member of the Lombard League in 1167, an alliance of northern Italian towns against the Holy Roman Emperor Frederick I Barbarossa.

The Bonacolsi family seized control of Mantua in 1276, initiating a period of political stability that lasted until 1328, when the Gonzaga family took over. The Gonzaga dynasty transformed Mantua into a Renaissance jewel, fostering a flourishing cultural scene that attracted artists, architects, and scholars. The construction of grand palaces, churches, and public buildings under the Gonzagas left an indelible mark on the city's architectural landscape.

Mantua's strategic importance continued into the modern era. In 1707, it became part of the Austrian Habsburg Empire and was heavily fortified as part of the Quadrilateral, a defensive network of fortresses. Napoleon captured the city in 1797, and it remained under French control until 1814, when it was returned to Austria. Mantua played a significant role in the Risorgimento, the movement for Italian unification, and joined the Kingdom of Italy in 1866.

Mantua is accessible via various modes of transportation, making it a convenient destination for travellers from different parts of Italy and Europe.

By Air:
The nearest major airport is Verona Villafranca Airport (VRN), located about 45 kilometres (28 miles) from Mantua. From the airport, visitors can reach Mantua by taxi, rental car, or shuttle bus to Verona Porta Nuova railway station, followed by a train to Mantua.

By Train:
Mantua is well-connected by rail, with frequent train services to and from major Italian cities. The city is served by the Mantua railway station (Stazione di Mantova), which is a hub for regional and intercity trains. Direct trains from Verona take approximately 45 minutes, while trains from Milan, Bologna, and Venice take around 1.5 to 2 hours. For travellers coming from Rome or Florence, a transfer in Bologna or Verona is usually required.

By Car:

Driving to Mantua is a feasible option, especially for those who wish to explore the surrounding countryside and nearby attractions. The city is accessible via the A22 Autostrada, which connects to major highways such as the A1 and A4. Parking is available in several locations around the city centre, although it is advisable to check for any restricted traffic zones (ZTL) before planning your route.

By Bus:
Long-distance buses and regional coach services also connect Mantua to various cities and towns in the region. Bus travel can be an economical option, although it may take longer than train travel.

By Bicycle:
For the more adventurous, cycling to Mantua can be a rewarding experience. The city is connected to several scenic bike routes, including the Mincio Cycle Path, which links Mantua to Peschiera del Garda, offering stunning views of the countryside and river along the way.

Mantua's climate is characterised by hot summers and cool winters, with distinct seasonal variations that influence the best times to visit.

Spring (March to May):
Spring is one of the best times to visit Mantua, as the weather is mild and pleasant, with temperatures ranging from 10°C to 20°C (50°F to 68°F). The city's gardens and parks come to life with blooming flowers, making it an ideal season for outdoor activities and sightseeing. Spring also marks the beginning of many cultural events and festivals.

Summer (June to August):
Summers in Mantua can be hot and humid, with temperatures often exceeding 30°C (86°F). While this season is popular with tourists, it is essential to stay hydrated and take breaks during the hottest part of the day. Despite the heat, summer is a lively time in Mantua, with numerous festivals, open-air concerts, and outdoor dining experiences.

Autumn (September to November):
Autumn is another excellent time to visit Mantua, with cooler temperatures ranging from 10°C to 20°C (50°F to 68°F). The fall foliage adds a beautiful

backdrop to the city's historic streets and buildings. This season is also harvest time, offering visitors the chance to sample fresh local produce and participate in food festivals.

Winter (December to February):
Winters in Mantua are cold, with temperatures occasionally dropping below freezing. While the weather can be less predictable, winter offers a quieter and more serene atmosphere. Visitors can enjoy indoor attractions such as museums, galleries, and historic sites without the crowds. The city's Christmas markets and holiday decorations add a festive charm to the winter season.

Mantua is a city of immense historical and cultural richness, easily accessible by various modes of transportation, and best visited during the milder seasons of spring and autumn. Whether exploring its Renaissance architecture, enjoying its vibrant cultural scene, or savouring its culinary delights, Mantua offers a captivating experience for travellers.

Chapter 1

Historical and Cultural Overview

Early History and Roman Influence

Mantua's early history is deeply intertwined with the civilizations that inhabited the region long before it became part of the Roman Empire. The area was originally settled by the Etruscans, an ancient civilization known for its sophisticated culture and significant influence on Roman society. The Etruscans established Mantua as a strategic settlement due to its advantageous position near the Mincio River, which provided both a natural defence and a means of transport and trade.

Following the Etruscan period, the Gallic tribe known as the Cenomani inhabited the region. They were part of the larger Celtic population that spread across northern Italy and parts of Europe. The

Cenomani integrated with the local Etruscan inhabitants, contributing to the cultural and demographic landscape of early Mantua.

The turning point in Mantua's early history came around 220 BCE when the Romans began their expansion into the Po Valley. Mantua was incorporated into the Roman Republic as a colony. The Romans recognized the strategic importance of Mantua's location and its potential as a centre for agriculture and trade. They built roads, bridges, and fortifications, significantly enhancing the infrastructure of the city. Roman colonisation brought about a period of stability and prosperity, which allowed Mantua to grow both in population and economic strength.

One of the most notable figures from this period is the poet Virgil (Publius Vergilius Maro), who was born in 70 BCE in the nearby village of Andes (modern-day Pietole). Virgil is celebrated as one of Rome's greatest poets, renowned for his epic work, the Aeneid, which has had a lasting impact on Western literature. Virgil's connection to Mantua has immortalised the city in literary history, and his legacy is a source of local pride.

Throughout the Roman period, Mantua thrived as an agricultural hub, producing grains, wine, and other crops that were essential to the Roman economy. The city's integration into the Roman network facilitated cultural exchange and the dissemination of Roman laws, customs, and architectural styles. Roman influence is still evident in Mantua's urban layout and archaeological remains, which provide a glimpse into its ancient past.

The Gonzaga Era

The Gonzaga era represents the golden age of Mantua, during which the city reached the pinnacle of its political, cultural, and artistic achievements. The Gonzaga family came to power in 1328, when Luigi Gonzaga overthrew the ruling Bonacolsi family. This marked the beginning of a dynasty that would rule Mantua for nearly four centuries, transforming it into a Renaissance jewel.

Under the Gonzagas, Mantua experienced unprecedented growth and development. The family was known for its patronage of the arts and its efforts to cultivate a vibrant cultural environment. They commissioned some of the most prominent architects, artists, and scholars of the time, turning Mantua into a centre of Renaissance culture.

One of the most significant contributions of the Gonzaga family was the construction of grand architectural projects that still define the city's landscape today. The Ducal Palace (Palazzo Ducale) is perhaps the most famous example. This vast complex, which includes courtyards, gardens, and buildings, served as the residence of the Gonzaga rulers and a symbol of their power and wealth. The palace houses numerous works of art, including frescoes by Andrea Mantegna, whose masterpiece, the Camera degli Sposi (Bridal Chamber), is a highlight.

Another architectural marvel from this period is the Palazzo Te, designed by Giulio Romano in the early 16th century. This pleasure palace is renowned for its Mannerist architecture and elaborate interior decorations. The Palazzo Te exemplifies the Gonzagas' taste for innovation and luxury, as well as their desire to create spaces that reflected their status and sophistication.

In addition to their architectural patronage, the Gonzagas supported the development of music, literature, and science. The court of Mantua attracted composers like Claudio Monteverdi, whose work laid the foundations for modern opera, and scientists such as Leon Battista Alberti, who contributed to various fields of knowledge.

The Gonzaga era also saw Mantua become a significant political player in the region. Their diplomatic acumen ensured Mantua's survival and prosperity amidst the shifting dynamics of Italian and European politics.

The Gonzaga rule ended in 1707, but their legacy endures in the cultural and architectural heritage they left behind. Mantua's identity as a Renaissance city is deeply rooted in the achievements of the Gonzaga family, whose influence shaped the city's character and reputation.

Austrian and Napoleonic Influence

Following the decline of the Gonzaga dynasty, Mantua became part of the Austrian Habsburg Empire in 1707. This period marked a new chapter in the city's history, characterised by significant military and administrative changes. The Habsburgs recognized Mantua's strategic importance and incorporated it into their defensive network known as the Quadrilateral, which also included the fortresses of Verona, Peschiera del Garda, and Legnago.

Under Austrian rule, Mantua was heavily fortified. The existing mediaeval and Renaissance fortifications were expanded and modernised to create a formidable defence system. These fortifications played a crucial role in maintaining Habsburg control over northern Italy and deterring potential invaders.

The city's military significance was highlighted during the Napoleonic Wars. In 1796, Napoleon Bonaparte launched his Italian campaign, aiming to disrupt Austrian dominance in the region. Mantua, with its strategic position and strong fortifications, became a focal point of the conflict. After a prolonged siege that lasted from June 1796 to February 1797, Napoleon's forces successfully captured Mantua. The city's fall was a significant victory for Napoleon, solidifying his control over northern Italy.

Napoleon's rule brought about administrative and social reforms that aimed to modernise Mantua and integrate it into the French Empire. These reforms included the introduction of the Napoleonic Code, which standardised laws and legal procedures. The French administration also undertook public works projects to improve infrastructure and urban planning.

However, Napoleon's dominance was short-lived. Following his defeat and the Congress of Vienna in 1814, Mantua was returned to Austrian control. The city remained under Austrian rule until the unification of Italy in the mid-19th century. During this period, Mantua continued to serve as a key military stronghold, but it also began to experience the early stirrings of the Risorgimento, the movement for Italian unification.

Mantua in Modern Times

The unification of Italy in 1866 brought Mantua into a new era as part of the Kingdom of Italy. The city's military role diminished, and it began to focus more on cultural and economic development. The late 19th and early 20th centuries saw the growth of Mantua's industrial sector, with the establishment of factories and the expansion of agricultural production.

Mantua's cultural heritage continued to be a source of pride and identity. The city preserved and restored many of its historic buildings, ensuring that the legacy of its past remained intact. This commitment to heritage preservation was recognized in 2008 when Mantua, along with the nearby town of Sabbioneta, was designated a UNESCO World Heritage site. This designation highlighted the city's exceptional Renaissance architecture and urban planning.

In modern times, Mantua has become a vibrant cultural destination, attracting visitors from around the world. The city hosts numerous festivals, exhibitions, and events that celebrate its rich history and artistic achievements. The Festivaletteratura, an annual literary festival, is one of the most prominent events, drawing writers, intellectuals, and readers to the city for a week of discussions, readings, and cultural activities.

Mantua's economy is now diverse, with a mix of agriculture, industry, and tourism. The city is known for its production of traditional foods, including pumpkin tortelli, risotto alla pilota, and sbrisolona (a type of crumbly cake). These culinary traditions, along with its historical and cultural attractions, make Mantua a unique and appealing destination.

Chapter 2

Exploring the City Center

Piazza Sordello

Piazza Sordello is the historical and cultural heart of Mantua, serving as a starting point for exploring the city's rich heritage. Named after the 13th-century troubadour Sordello da Goito, the square is surrounded by some of Mantua's most significant architectural and historical landmarks. Piazza Sordello's spacious and elegant layout provides a perfect setting for appreciating the grandeur of Mantua's past.

Location and How to Get There:
Piazza Sordello is situated in the city centre, easily accessible by foot from other major attractions. If arriving by train, it is a short walk from Mantua railway station. The square can also be reached by local buses that stop nearby. For those driving, there are parking facilities around the city centre, but it is

advisable to check for any traffic restrictions in the historical zone.

Features and Significance:
The square's northern side is dominated by the imposing Ducal Palace (Palazzo Ducale), a vast complex that served as the residence of the Gonzaga family. The western side features the majestic Mantua Cathedral (Cattedrale di San Pietro), while the eastern side is lined with historic buildings, including the Bishop's Palace. The open space of Piazza Sordello is often used for public events, markets, and festivals, adding to its vibrant atmosphere.

Walking through Piazza Sordello, visitors can sense the layers of history that have shaped Mantua. The square's cobblestone pavement, historic facades, and architectural diversity reflect the city's evolution from a mediaeval stronghold to a Renaissance masterpiece. The piazza is an ideal place to start a tour of Mantua, offering a panoramic view of the city's architectural and cultural treasures.

The Ducal Palace

The Ducal Palace, also known as Palazzo Ducale, is one of Mantua's most iconic landmarks. This vast architectural complex served as the residence and administrative centre of the powerful Gonzaga family, who ruled Mantua for nearly four centuries. The palace is a testament to the family's wealth, influence, and patronage of the arts.

Location and How to Get There:
The Ducal Palace is located on the northern side of Piazza Sordello, making it easily accessible from other central attractions. It is a short walk from the Mantua railway station and can be reached by local buses that stop near Piazza Sordello. For those driving, there are parking facilities in the vicinity, but visitors should check for any restricted traffic zones.

Architectural and Historical Highlights:
The Ducal Palace complex covers an area of approximately 34,000 square metres, encompassing a series of interconnected buildings, courtyards, and gardens. It includes the Corte Vecchia (Old Court),

the Corte Nuova (New Court), and the Castello di San Giorgio, among other sections. Each part of the palace showcases different architectural styles and historical periods.

One of the most famous features of the Ducal Palace is the Camera degli Sposi (Bridal Chamber), located in the Castello di San Giorgio. This room, decorated with frescoes by Andrea Mantegna, is considered a masterpiece of Renaissance art. The frescoes depict scenes from the life of the Gonzaga family and demonstrate Mantegna's skill in creating realistic, three-dimensional effects.

Other notable areas within the palace include the Sala del Pisanello, adorned with frescoes by the artist Pisanello, and the Sala degli Specchi (Hall of Mirrors), which reflects the opulence of the Gonzaga court. The palace also houses a rich collection of paintings, sculptures, tapestries, and other works of art, many of which were commissioned by the Gonzagas.

Visitors to the Ducal Palace can explore its grand rooms, intricate decorations, and beautiful gardens, gaining insight into the life and legacy of the

Gonzaga family. The palace's diverse architecture and art make it a key destination for anyone interested in Renaissance history and culture.

Mantua Cathedral

Mantua Cathedral, or Cattedrale di San Pietro, is a prominent religious and architectural landmark in the city. The cathedral's history dates back to early Christian times, although it has undergone numerous renovations and reconstructions over the centuries. Today, it stands as a symbol of Mantua's religious heritage and architectural evolution.

Location and How to Get There:
Mantua Cathedral is located on the western side of Piazza Sordello, directly opposite the Ducal Palace. Its central location makes it easily accessible on foot from other nearby attractions. Visitors arriving by train can reach the cathedral with a short walk from the Mantua railway station, while local buses also stop near Piazza Sordello. Parking facilities are available in the vicinity for those travelling by car.

Architectural and Historical Highlights:

The current structure of Mantua Cathedral reflects a mix of architectural styles, primarily Renaissance and Baroque, resulting from various phases of reconstruction. The cathedral's facade, designed by the architect Giovanni Battista Bertani in the 16th century, is a striking example of Renaissance architecture, characterised by its harmonious proportions and classical elements.

Inside the cathedral, visitors can admire the richly decorated interior, featuring a combination of Renaissance and Baroque art and architecture. The nave is flanked by side chapels adorned with frescoes, altarpieces, and sculptures. One of the most notable features is the chapel dedicated to Saint Anselm, which contains relics of the saint and beautifully crafted decorations.

The cathedral's dome, a later addition, was designed by the architect Filippo Juvarra in the 18th century. The dome's Baroque design adds to the grandeur of the interior, with its intricate stuccoes and frescoes. The cathedral also houses several important works of art, including paintings by local and regional artists.

Mantua Cathedral continues to serve as a place of worship and a centre for religious and community activities. Its historical and artistic significance makes it a must-visit site for those exploring Mantua's rich cultural heritage.

Church of San Andrea

The Church of San Andrea, or Basilica di Sant'Andrea, is one of Mantua's most important religious buildings and a masterpiece of Renaissance architecture. Designed by the renowned architect Leon Battista Alberti, the church is renowned for its harmonious proportions and innovative design.

Location and How to Get There:
The Church of San Andrea is located in Piazza Mantegna, a short walk from Piazza Sordello and other central attractions. It is easily accessible from the Mantua railway station and by local buses that stop nearby. For those driving, parking facilities are

available in the area, although it is advisable to check for any traffic restrictions.

Architectural and Historical Highlights:
Construction of the Church of San Andrea began in 1472, although it was completed several decades later. Alberti's design reflects his deep understanding of classical architecture and his innovative approach to church design. The church's facade is characterised by its grandeur and simplicity, with a large central arch flanked by Corinthian pilasters.

The interior of the church is equally impressive, featuring a Latin cross plan with a single nave and side chapels. The nave's vaulted ceiling and large arches create a sense of spaciousness and light. One of the most significant features of the church is the crypt, which houses relics traditionally believed to be the blood of Christ, collected by the Roman centurion Longinus.

The Chapel of St. Longinus, in particular, is adorned with Mantegna's frescoes depicting scenes from the life of Christ and the Passion.

The Church of San Andrea remains an active place of worship and a key site for pilgrims and art enthusiasts. Its architectural and artistic treasures offer a glimpse into the religious and cultural life of Renaissance Mantua.

Rotonda di San Lorenzo

The Rotonda di San Lorenzo is Mantua's oldest church, dating back to the late 11th century. This circular Romanesque structure is a remarkable example of early mediaeval architecture and holds significant historical and religious importance.

Location and How to Get There:
The Rotonda di San Lorenzo is located in Piazza delle Erbe, near the Palazzo della Ragione and the Torre dell'Orologio. It is within walking distance of Piazza Sordello and other central attractions. Visitors can reach the church from the Mantua railway station with a short walk or by using local buses that stop nearby. Parking facilities are available in the area for those travelling by car.

Architectural and Historical Highlights:

The Rotonda di San Lorenzo was built in the late 11th century, inspired by the Church of the Holy Sepulchre in Jerusalem. Its circular design and central plan are characteristic of Romanesque architecture, reflecting the influence of early Christian and Byzantine church designs.

The church's interior is simple yet evocative, with a central nave surrounded by an ambulatory and topped by a domed roof. The walls are adorned with fragments of frescoes, some of which date back to the mediaeval period. These frescoes, although partially damaged, provide valuable insights into the artistic styles and religious themes of the time.

Over the centuries, the Rotonda di San Lorenzo fell into disrepair and was even used for secular purposes before being restored in the 20th century. Today, it stands as a testament to Mantua's mediaeval heritage and early Christian architectural traditions.

Visitors to the Rotonda di San Lorenzo can explore its unique design and appreciate its historical significance. The church's serene atmosphere and ancient walls offer a glimpse into Mantua's distant past, making it a compelling destination for history enthusiasts and those interested in mediaeval architecture.

Mantua offers a journey through time, from its mediaeval origins to its Renaissance splendour. Piazza Sordello, the Ducal Palace, Mantua Cathedral, the Church of San Andrea, and the Rotonda di San Lorenzo each provide unique insights into the city's rich historical and cultural heritage. Visitors can immerse themselves in the architectural beauty and artistic achievements that define Mantua, gaining a deeper appreciation for this remarkable city.

Chapter 3

Museums and Art Galleries

Museo di Palazzo Ducale

The Museo di Palazzo Ducale, housed within the grand Ducal Palace complex, is one of Mantua's most significant cultural institutions. This museum offers a comprehensive insight into the history, art, and architecture of the Gonzaga dynasty and their extensive patronage.

Location:
The Museo di Palazzo Ducale is located in Piazza Sordello, at the heart of Mantua's historic centre. This central location makes it easily accessible by foot from other notable attractions. Visitors arriving by train can reach the museum with a short walk from the Mantua railway station. Local buses also stop near Piazza Sordello, and parking facilities are available in the vicinity for those travelling by car.

Historical and Artistic Highlights:
The museum spans a vast area, including the old and new courts of the Ducal Palace and the Castello di San Giorgio. This architectural complex, covering approximately 34,000 square metres, features a series of interconnected buildings, courtyards, and gardens.

One of the most famous sections of the museum is the Camera degli Sposi, or the Bridal Chamber, located in the Castello di San Giorgio. This room, adorned with frescoes by Andrea Mantegna, is a masterpiece of Renaissance art. The frescoes depict scenes from the life of the Gonzaga family, showcasing Mantegna's skill in creating realistic, three-dimensional effects.

The museum's extensive collection includes works of art, tapestries, sculptures, and furniture from various periods. The Sala del Pisanello features frescoes by the artist Pisanello, while the Sala degli Specchi (Hall of Mirrors) reflects the opulence of the Gonzaga court. Visitors can explore the grand rooms, intricate decorations, and beautiful gardens, gaining insight into the life and legacy of the Gonzaga family.

In addition to its permanent collections, the museum also hosts temporary exhibitions and cultural events, making it a dynamic centre for art and history. The Museo di Palazzo Ducale is a must-visit destination for anyone interested in Renaissance history and culture.

Museo di Palazzo Te

The Museo di Palazzo Te is another of Mantua's premier cultural attractions, housed within the Palazzo Te, a masterpiece of Renaissance architecture designed by Giulio Romano. This museum offers a unique blend of art, history, and architectural innovation.

Location:
The Museo di Palazzo Te is situated in Viale Te, just outside the historical centre of Mantua. It is easily accessible by foot or a short bus ride from the city centre. For those arriving by train, the museum is a short taxi ride from the Mantua railway station.

Parking facilities are available nearby for visitors travelling by car.

Architectural and Artistic Highlights:
Palazzo Te was built between 1525 and 1535 as a pleasure palace for Federico II Gonzaga. Giulio Romano, a pupil of Raphael, designed the palace with a blend of classical and innovative architectural elements. The building's layout includes a series of courtyards, gardens, and grand halls, each adorned with elaborate frescoes and decorations.

The Sala dei Giganti (Hall of the Giants) is one of the most famous rooms in the palace, featuring dramatic frescoes depicting the fall of the giants from Greek mythology. The frescoes cover the entire room, creating an immersive and dynamic visual experience.

Another highlight is the Sala di Amore e Psiche (Room of Love and Psyche), which showcases frescoes depicting the mythological tale of Cupid and Psyche. These frescoes, with their vivid colours and intricate details, are a testament to Giulio Romano's artistic genius.

The museum's collections include paintings, sculptures, and decorative arts from the Renaissance period. Visitors can explore the grand rooms, admire the intricate frescoes, and stroll through the beautifully landscaped gardens, gaining a deeper understanding of the cultural and artistic achievements of the Gonzaga court.

The Museo di Palazzo Te also hosts temporary exhibitions, cultural events, and educational programs, making it a vibrant centre for art and history. Its architectural beauty and artistic treasures make it a key destination for visitors to Mantua.

Accademia Virgiliana

The Accademia Virgiliana, also known as the Accademia Nazionale Virgiliana, is an important cultural and educational institution in Mantua, named in honour of the great Latin poet Virgil, who was born near Mantua. The academy plays a significant role in promoting the arts, sciences, and literature.

Location:

The Accademia Virgiliana is located in Via Accademia, in the historic centre of Mantua. It is easily accessible on foot from other central attractions, such as Piazza Sordello and the Ducal Palace. Visitors arriving by train can reach the academy with a short walk from the Mantua railway station. Local buses also stop nearby, and parking facilities are available in the vicinity for those travelling by car.

Historical and Cultural Significance:

Founded in 1768 by Empress Maria Theresa of Austria, the Accademia Virgiliana has a long history of fostering intellectual and cultural pursuits. The academy's headquarters, housed in a historic building, includes a concert hall, a library, and various meeting rooms.

One of the key features of the Accademia Virgiliana is the Scientific Theatre, designed by the architect Antonio Bibiena in 1769. The theatre is renowned for its acoustics and elegant design, with a horseshoe-shaped auditorium and richly decorated interior. It has hosted numerous concerts, lectures, and performances, contributing to Mantua's vibrant cultural scene.

The academy's library contains a valuable collection of books, manuscripts, and documents, including rare editions of works by Virgil and other classical authors. Researchers and scholars can access these resources for academic and literary studies.

In addition to its educational activities, the Accademia Virgiliana organises conferences, exhibitions, and cultural events, promoting the exchange of ideas and knowledge. The academy's role in preserving and celebrating Mantua's intellectual heritage makes it a key cultural institution in the city.

Visitors to the Accademia Virgiliana can explore its historic building, attend cultural events, and delve into its rich collections, gaining insight into the intellectual and artistic life of Mantua.

State Archives and Library

The State Archives and Library of Mantua, known as Archivio di Stato di Mantova, is a vital institution for the preservation and study of the city's historical documents and literary treasures. The archives and library offer valuable resources for researchers, historians, and visitors interested in Mantua's rich past.

Location:
The State Archives and Library are located in Via Roberto Ardigò, in the historic centre of Mantua. They are easily accessible by foot from other central attractions, such as Piazza Sordello and the Ducal Palace. Visitors arriving by train can reach the archives with a short walk from the Mantua railway station. Local buses also stop nearby, and parking facilities are available in the vicinity for those travelling by car.

Historical and Cultural Significance:
The State Archives of Mantua house a vast collection of documents, manuscripts, and records dating back to the mediaeval period. These archives provide a comprehensive overview of Mantua's political, social, and cultural history. The documents include official records of the Gonzaga family, legal

documents, letters, and administrative records, offering a wealth of information for historical research.

The library's collection includes rare books, manuscripts, and incunabula (early printed books), with a particular focus on works related to Mantua and the Gonzaga dynasty. Among its treasures are illuminated manuscripts, early editions of classical texts, and historical maps. The library's reading rooms provide a quiet and conducive environment for study and research.

The State Archives and Library also play a crucial role in preserving Mantua's cultural heritage through conservation and digitization projects. These efforts ensure that valuable historical documents and books are preserved for future generations and made accessible to a wider audience.

In addition to its archival and library functions, the institution organises exhibitions, lectures, and educational programs, highlighting various aspects of Mantua's history and culture. These events provide opportunities for the public to engage with the city's rich heritage and learn more about its historical significance.

Visitors to the State Archives and Library can explore its extensive collections, attend cultural events, and gain a deeper understanding of Mantua's historical and literary legacy. The institution's dedication to preserving and promoting Mantua's heritage makes it an essential destination for anyone interested in the city's past.

Mantua's museums and art galleries offer a rich tapestry of art, history, and culture. The Museo di Palazzo Ducale, Museo di Palazzo Te, Accademia Virgiliana, and the State Archives and Library each provide unique insights into the city's heritage. Visitors can explore grand palaces, admire Renaissance masterpieces, delve into historical documents, and engage with Mantua's vibrant cultural life, gaining a deeper appreciation for this remarkable city.

Chapter 4

Architectural Highlights

Castello di San Giorgio

The Castello di San Giorgio, part of the expansive Ducal Palace complex, is one of Mantua's most iconic landmarks. This castle is a testament to the city's rich history, blending mediaeval military architecture with Renaissance artistry.

Location:
The Castello di San Giorgio is situated on the northeastern edge of Mantua's historic centre, within the Ducal Palace complex. Its proximity to Piazza Sordello makes it easily accessible on foot from other key attractions in the city. Visitors arriving by train can reach the castle with a short walk from the Mantua railway station. Local buses also stop near Piazza Sordello, and parking facilities are available nearby for those travelling by car.

Historical and Architectural Significance:

Constructed between 1395 and 1406 by Bartolino da Novara under the commission of Francesco I Gonzaga, the castle originally served a defensive purpose. Its robust square plan, fortified walls, and corner towers exemplify the military architecture of the late mediaeval period. A moat, which once encircled the castle, added to its defensive capabilities, and three drawbridges provided controlled access.

In the early 15th century, under Ludovico II Gonzaga, the castle's function transitioned from a fortress to a more residential and ceremonial role. This transformation marked the beginning of the castle's Renaissance phase. The most notable feature of this period is the Camera degli Sposi (Bridal Chamber), also known as the Camera Picta, a room adorned with frescoes by Andrea Mantegna. Completed between 1465 and 1474, these frescoes depict scenes from the lives of the Gonzaga family, including courtly life and notable events. Mantegna's use of perspective and his attention to detail make these frescoes masterpieces of Renaissance art.

The castle's upper levels were later used as a high-security prison during Austrian rule in the 18th and 19th centuries, further adding to its complex history. Today, the Castello di San Giorgio is a key part of the Museo di Palazzo Ducale, allowing visitors to explore its historical and artistic treasures.

Palazzo del Te

Palazzo del Te is one of Mantua's most celebrated architectural achievements, designed by Giulio Romano for Federico II Gonzaga as a suburban villa. This palazzo exemplifies the elegance and innovation of Renaissance architecture.

Location:
Palazzo del Te is located in Viale Te, just outside the historical centre of Mantua. It is easily accessible by foot or a short bus ride from the city centre. For those arriving by train, the palazzo is a short taxi ride from the Mantua railway station. Parking facilities are available nearby for visitors travelling by car.

Architectural and Artistic Significance:
Built between 1525 and 1535, Palazzo del Te was designed as a retreat for the Gonzaga family, intended for leisure and entertainment rather than as a permanent residence. Giulio Romano, a pupil of Raphael, employed a combination of classical and Mannerist elements in the design, creating a structure that is both harmonious and innovative.

The building's layout includes a series of courtyards, gardens, and grand halls, each adorned with elaborate frescoes and decorations. The Sala dei Giganti (Hall of the Giants) is one of the most famous rooms in the palazzo, featuring dramatic frescoes depicting the fall of the giants from Greek mythology. The frescoes cover the entire room, creating an immersive and dynamic visual experience.

Another highlight is the Sala di Amore e Psiche (Room of Love and Psyche), which showcases frescoes depicting the mythological tale of Cupid and Psyche. These frescoes, with their vivid colours and intricate details, are a testament to Giulio Romano's artistic genius.

The palazzo's architecture and decorations reflect Gonzaga's taste for classical mythology, luxury, and artistic innovation. Visitors can explore the grand rooms, admire the intricate frescoes, and stroll through the beautifully landscaped gardens, gaining a deeper understanding of the cultural and artistic achievements of the Gonzaga court.

Palazzo della Ragione

Palazzo della Ragione is one of Mantua's oldest and most significant civic buildings. This mediaeval structure has played a central role in the city's public and judicial life for centuries.

Location:
Palazzo della Ragione is located in Piazza delle Erbe, one of Mantua's main squares. Its central location makes it easily accessible on foot from other key attractions in the city. Visitors arriving by train can reach the palazzo with a short walk from the Mantua railway station. Local buses also stop

near Piazza delle Erbe, and parking facilities are available nearby for those travelling by car.

Historical and Architectural Significance:
The palazzo was constructed in the late 12th century and has undergone various modifications and restorations over the centuries. Its original purpose was to serve as a courthouse and a venue for civic assemblies, reflecting its name, which translates to "Palace of Reason."

The building's architecture is characterised by its Romanesque and Gothic elements, with a large hall on the upper floor and an open loggia on the ground floor. The loggia, supported by a series of arches, provided a sheltered space for market activities and public gatherings.

One of the most notable features of the Palazzo della Ragione is the Torre dell'Orologio (Clock Tower), added in the 15th century. The clock tower, with its distinctive astronomical clock, has become an iconic symbol of Mantua. The clock, designed by Bartolomeo Manfredi, displays the time, the phases of the moon, and the positions of the sun and stars, reflecting the Renaissance fascination with astronomy and science.

Inside the palazzo, visitors can explore the grand hall, which has been used for various purposes over the centuries, including as a courtroom, a market hall, and an exhibition space. The hall's frescoed walls, depicting scenes from Mantua's history and mythology, add to the building's historical and artistic significance.

Palazzo della Ragione continues to play a role in Mantua's cultural life, hosting exhibitions, events, and public functions. Its architectural beauty and historical importance make it a key destination for visitors to the city.

San Sebastiano and San Francesco Churches

The churches of San Sebastiano and San Francesco are among Mantua's most important religious and architectural landmarks, each reflecting different periods and styles in the city's history.

San Sebastiano:

Location:

The Church of San Sebastiano is located in Viale San Sebastiano, on the eastern edge of Mantua's historic centre. It is easily accessible by foot from other central attractions, such as the Ducal Palace and Piazza Sordello. Visitors arriving by train can reach the church with a short walk from the Mantua railway station. Local buses also stop nearby, and parking facilities are available in the vicinity for those travelling by car.

Architectural and Historical Significance:

San Sebastiano was designed by the renowned Renaissance architect Leon Battista Alberti and constructed between 1460 and 1470. Alberti's design reflects the principles of classical architecture, with a focus on symmetry, proportion, and harmony.

The church's facade is characterised by its geometric simplicity and elegant proportions, with a central pediment supported by pilasters. The interior, though relatively austere, showcases Alberti's mastery of spatial design, with a clear and harmonious layout.

San Sebastiano was intended as a mausoleum for the Gonzaga family, and its design includes a crypt where members of the family were to be buried. The church's architectural purity and historical significance make it an important example of Renaissance ecclesiastical architecture.

San Francesco:

Location:
The Church of San Francesco is located in Via Antonio Giuseppe Bertani, in the northeastern part of Mantua's historic centre. It is easily accessible on foot from other key attractions, such as the Castello di San Giorgio and Piazza Sordello. Visitors arriving by train can reach the church with a short walk from the Mantua railway station. Local buses also stop nearby, and parking facilities are available in the vicinity for those travelling by car.

Architectural and Historical Significance:
San Francesco was founded in 1304 and reflects the Gothic architectural style that was prevalent in Italy

during the late mediaeval period. The church's facade, with its pointed arches and rose window, exemplifies the Gothic aesthetic.

The interior of San Francesco is characterised by its spacious nave and side aisles, supported by slender columns. The church's vaulted ceilings and large windows create a sense of verticality and light, typical of Gothic architecture.

San Francesco has undergone various modifications and restorations over the centuries, but it retains many of its original Gothic features. The church also houses important works of art, including frescoes and altarpieces from different periods.

Both San Sebastiano and San Francesco reflect the rich religious and architectural heritage of Mantua, offering visitors insight into different styles and periods of the city's history. Their architectural beauty and historical significance make them key destinations for anyone exploring Mantua's cultural and religious landscape.

Mantua's architectural highlights, including the Castello di San Giorgio, Palazzo del Te, Palazzo della Ragione, and the churches of San Sebastiano and San Francesco, offer a rich tapestry of history, art, and architectural innovation. These landmarks provide a comprehensive view of Mantua's evolution over the centuries, from its mediaeval roots to its Renaissance grandeur and beyond. Visitors to Mantua can immerse themselves in the city's architectural beauty, gaining a deeper appreciation for its cultural and historical significance.

Chapter 5

Parks and Outdoor Activities

Parco del Mincio

Parco del Mincio, or Mincio Park, is a natural oasis that spans across the Lombardy region, offering a haven for nature enthusiasts and a respite from the urban environment. The park encompasses a diverse range of ecosystems, from wetlands and lakes to forests and agricultural lands, all connected by the Mincio River. This extensive natural reserve plays a crucial role in preserving the region's biodiversity and providing recreational opportunities for both locals and visitors.

Location:
Parco del Mincio stretches from the town of Peschiera del Garda, where the Mincio River flows out of Lake Garda, down to the city of Mantua. The park is easily accessible from Mantua, with multiple

entry points along its length. The main visitor centre is located near the town of Rivalta sul Mincio, which can be reached by car or public transport from Mantua.

Ecological Significance:

The park's diverse habitats support a rich variety of flora and fauna, making it an important site for conservation. Wetlands, such as those found around the Valli del Mincio, are home to numerous bird species, including herons, egrets, and various migratory birds. The lakes and river provide habitats for fish, amphibians, and aquatic plants, while the surrounding forests and meadows support mammals, insects, and a wide range of plant species.

The park's management focuses on maintaining and enhancing these natural habitats through various conservation projects. Efforts include the restoration of wetlands, the creation of artificial islands for bird nesting, and the management of water levels to support diverse ecosystems. These initiatives not only protect wildlife but also improve the quality of the environment for human visitors.

Recreational Opportunities:

Parco del Mincio offers a multitude of recreational activities that allow visitors to experience its natural beauty. Birdwatching is a popular activity, with several observation points and hides located throughout the park. Guided nature walks and educational tours are available, providing insights into the park's ecology and conservation efforts.

The park's network of trails is ideal for hiking and cycling, with paths ranging from easy walks to more challenging routes. These trails wind through different landscapes, offering scenic views of the river, lakes, and wetlands. Visitors can also explore the park by canoe or kayak, paddling along the Mincio River and its tributaries.

For those interested in history and culture, the park includes several historical sites, such as the ancient town of Borghetto and the mediaeval fortifications of Valeggio sul Mincio. These sites add a cultural dimension to the natural beauty of the park, making it a well-rounded destination for all types of visitors.

Cycling and Walking Trails

Mantua and its surrounding areas are renowned for their extensive network of cycling and walking trails, which cater to a variety of fitness levels and interests. These trails provide an excellent way to explore the region's natural landscapes, historical sites, and charming villages, all while enjoying the fresh air and scenic views.

Location and Accessibility:
The trails in and around Mantua are well-marked and easily accessible from the city centre. Key starting points include the Parco del Mincio, the historic centre of Mantua, and various villages along the Mincio River. Many trails intersect with public transport routes, allowing visitors to combine different modes of travel. Bike rental shops are available in Mantua and other towns, providing bicycles and equipment for all ages and preferences.

Popular Trails:
1. Mincio Cycle Path: One of the most popular routes, the Mincio Cycle Path runs from Peschiera del Garda to Mantua, following the course of the

Mincio River. This 43-kilometre trail is relatively flat and well-maintained, making it suitable for cyclists of all skill levels. Along the way, riders can enjoy views of the river, wetlands, and rural landscapes, as well as stop at picturesque villages and historical sites.

2. Mantua City Trails: Within Mantua itself, several walking and cycling paths connect the city's main attractions. These urban trails take visitors past landmarks such as the Ducal Palace, Piazza Sordello, and the Castello di San Giorgio, as well as along the shores of the city's surrounding lakes. The combination of urban scenery and natural beauty makes these trails a pleasant way to explore Mantua on foot or by bike.

3. Rural and Scenic Routes: Beyond the Mincio Cycle Path, numerous other trails wind through the countryside around Mantua. These routes offer a mix of paved paths and gravel tracks, passing through fields, forests, and along the banks of smaller rivers and canals. Trails such as the "Strada del Riso" (Rice Road) and the "Strada del Vino e dei Sapori Mantovani" (Mantuan Wine and Flavors

Road) combine natural scenery with opportunities to sample local agricultural products and wines.

Amenities and Services:
The cycling and walking trails are supported by a range of amenities, including rest areas, picnic spots, and information boards. Cafes, restaurants, and agriturismos (farm stays) along the routes offer refreshments and accommodation, allowing visitors to plan multi-day trips. Guided tours and organised group rides are also available, providing additional support and local knowledge.

Safety is a priority on these trails, with clear signage, well-maintained surfaces, and measures in place to ensure the well-being of cyclists and walkers. Maps and route information are readily available from tourist offices and online resources, helping visitors to plan their excursions.

Boat Tours on the Mincio River

Exploring the Mincio River by boat offers a unique perspective on the natural and cultural landscape of Mantua and its surroundings. Boat tours provide an opportunity to experience the tranquillity of the river, observe wildlife, and learn about the region's history and ecology from a different vantage point.

Location and Tour Options:
Boat tours typically depart from the docks near Mantua's historic center, with various operators offering different types of excursions. These tours can range from short, hour-long trips around the city's lakes to longer journeys that explore the broader Mincio River and its wetlands. Some tours also include stops at key points of interest, such as the Parco del Mincio and the village of Grazie, known for its Sanctuary of Our Lady of Grace.

Tour Highlights:
1. City Lakes Tour: A popular option is a tour of Mantua's three lakes – Lago Superiore, Lago daai Mezzo, and Lago Inferiore. These lakes, formed by the Mincio River, encircle the city on three sides, creating a picturesque setting. The tour provides stunning views of Mantua's skyline, including landmarks such as the Ducal Palace, the Castello di

San Giorgio, and the Basilica of Sant'Andrea. The serene waters and the backdrop of historic architecture make this tour a highlight for many visitors.

2. Natural and Wildlife Tours: For those interested in nature, longer boat tours venture into the wetlands and nature reserves of the Parco del Mincio. These tours often include guided commentary on the area's flora and fauna, with opportunities to spot birds, fish, and other wildlife. The Valli del Mincio, with its marshes and reed beds, is a particularly rich area for birdwatching, hosting species such as herons, kingfishers, and migratory birds.

3. Cultural and Historical Tours: Some boat tours combine natural beauty with cultural exploration, visiting historical sites along the river. For example, tours may include a stop at the Sanctuary of Our Lady of Grace in the village of Grazie, a significant pilgrimage site with a rich history and unique interior decorations. These tours often provide insights into the historical and cultural significance of the river and its surroundings.

Amenities and Services:

Boat tours are generally well-equipped, with comfortable seating, informative guides, and safety measures in place. Many tours offer commentary in multiple languages, making them accessible to international visitors. Refreshments are often available on board, and some tours include meals or tastings of local products. Booking in advance is recommended, especially during peak tourist seasons, to secure a spot on the desired tour.

The Mincio Cycle Path

The Mincio Cycle Path is one of the most scenic and popular cycling routes in the Lombardy region, offering a leisurely way to explore the natural and cultural landscapes between Lake Garda and Mantua. This well-maintained path is ideal for cyclists of all ages and skill levels, providing a safe and enjoyable ride through picturesque countryside and along the banks of the Mincio River.

Location and Route Description:
The Mincio Cycle Path begins in Peschiera del Garda, a charming town on the southern shore of

Lake Garda. From there, it follows the course of the Mincio River southward to Mantua, covering a distance of approximately 43 kilometres. The path is predominantly flat and paved, making it accessible for both casual cyclists and families.

Scenic Highlights:

1. Lake Garda to Valeggio sul Mincio: The northern section of the path runs from Peschiera del Garda to the town of Valeggio sul Mincio. This stretch offers beautiful views of the river, lush green fields, and the fortified town of Borghetto sul Mincio, known for its mediaeval bridges and watermills. Borghetto is a popular stop for cyclists, with its quaint cafes and restaurants offering local delicacies.

2. Valeggio sul Mincio to Mantua: The southern section of the path continues from Valeggio sul Mincio to Mantua, passing through the Parco del Mincio. This area is characterised by its wetlands, reed beds, and diverse wildlife. Cyclists can enjoy the tranquillity of the natural surroundings, with opportunities to spot birds and other wildlife. As the path approaches Mantua, it offers views of the city's skyline and its surrounding lakes.

Amenities and Services:

The Mincio Cycle Path is well-equipped with amenities to support cyclists. Rest areas with benches, picnic spots, and water fountains are available along the route. Information boards provide maps and details about the local flora, fauna, and points of interest. Bike rental shops and repair stations are available in Peschiera del Garda and Mantua, offering a range of bicycles and equipment for hire.

For those planning longer trips, accommodation options such as hotels, B&Bs, and agriturismos are available along the route. Many of these establishments cater specifically to cyclists, providing secure bike storage and repair facilities. Guided tours and organised cycling events are also offered, providing additional support and local knowledge.

Safety and Accessibility:

Safety is a priority on the Mincio Cycle Path, with clear signage, well-maintained surfaces, and measures in place to ensure the well-being of cyclists. The path is separated from motor vehicle traffic for most of its length, providing a safe and peaceful ride. Maps and route information are readily available from tourist offices and online resources, helping visitors to plan their excursions.

Mantua and its surroundings offer a wealth of parks and outdoor activities, from the diverse ecosystems of Parco del Mincio to the scenic cycling and walking trails, boat tours on the Mincio River, and the popular Mincio Cycle Path. These outdoor experiences allow visitors to immerse themselves in the natural beauty and cultural heritage of the region, providing a refreshing and enriching complement to the city's historical and architectural attractions. Whether you are a nature lover, a cycling enthusiast, or simply looking for a relaxing way to explore the area, Mantua's parks and outdoor activities have something to offer for everyone.

Chapter 6

Day Trips and Surrounding Areas

Sabbioneta

Sabbioneta, a small town located approximately 30 kilometres east of Mantua, is renowned for its well-preserved Renaissance architecture and urban planning. Founded in the late 16th century by Vespasiano Gonzaga Colonna, Sabbioneta is a UNESCO World Heritage Site, celebrated for its unique design and historical significance. The town exemplifies the ideals of Renaissance urbanism and represents an important chapter in the history of northern Italy.

Location and Accessibility:
Sabbioneta is situated in the Lombardy region, within the province of Mantua. The town is easily accessible from Mantua by car, with a journey time

of around 30 minutes. Public transport options include regional trains and buses, which connect Mantua to Sabbioneta and offer a convenient alternative for visitors without private vehicles.

Historical and Architectural Significance:
Sabbioneta was meticulously planned and constructed by Vespasiano Gonzaga Colonna, who envisioned it as a model Renaissance city. The town's layout is characterised by its geometric precision and symmetry, reflecting the principles of Renaissance design. Key features of Sabbioneta include its fortified walls, gates, and a series of public and private buildings that demonstrate the grandeur of its era.

1. The Ducal Palace: This central building served as the residence of Vespasiano Gonzaga and his court. The palace is notable for its elegant architecture, which combines Renaissance and Mannerist styles. Visitors can explore its richly decorated rooms and admire the frescoes and artworks that adorn its walls.

2. The Olympic Theatre: Designed by the architect Vincenzo Scamozzi, the Olympic Theatre is a prime

example of Renaissance theatre design. It is renowned for its sophisticated stage machinery and acoustics, reflecting the importance of performing arts in Renaissance society. The theatre continues to host cultural events and performances, offering a glimpse into the artistic life of the period.

3. The Church of San Francesco: This church, with its simple yet elegant design, was an important religious centre in Sabbioneta. Its interior features Baroque elements and provides insight into the religious practices of the time.

4. The Walls and Gates: Sabbioneta is encircled by impressive fortifications, including the Porta Imperiale and Porta Vittoria. These defensive structures not only served practical purposes but also contributed to the town's aesthetic appeal.

Activities and Attractions:
Visitors to Sabbioneta can enjoy guided tours that provide historical context and insights into the town's development. Walking through the town's streets offers a sense of stepping back in time, with well-preserved buildings and public spaces that retain their Renaissance charm. The town also hosts

cultural events and festivals throughout the year, enhancing the visitor experience.

Amenities and Services:
Sabbioneta offers a range of amenities for visitors, including cafes, restaurants, and shops. Local establishments provide opportunities to sample regional cuisine and purchase souvenirs. The town's small size makes it easy to navigate on foot, and information centres are available to assist visitors with maps and details about the area's attractions.

Peschiera del Garda

Peschiera del Garda is a picturesque town located at the southern end of Lake Garda, approximately 40 kilometres west of Mantua. Known for its stunning lake views and historic fortifications, Peschiera del Garda is a popular destination for both relaxation and exploration. The town's strategic location on the lake's shores and its rich history make it a fascinating place to visit.

Location and Accessibility:

Peschiera del Garda is situated in the Veneto region, though it is close to the border with Lombardy. The town is accessible from Mantua by car, with a journey time of around 40 minutes. It can also be reached by train, with regular services connecting Mantua to Peschiera del Garda, making it a convenient day trip destination.

Historical and Cultural Significance:
Peschiera del Garda has a long history that dates back to Roman times. The town's fortifications, designed by the renowned architect Vauban, reflect its importance as a military and strategic location. The historic centre, with its charming canals and narrow streets, offers a glimpse into the town's past.

1. The Fortifications: Peschiera del Garda is renowned for its well-preserved fortifications, which include bastions, moats, and defensive walls. The fortifications are part of the Vauban Fortifications, a UNESCO World Heritage Site. Walking along the walls and exploring the bastions provides insight into the town's military history.

2. The Historic Centre: The town's historic centre is characterised by its picturesque canals, charming

piazzas, and historic buildings. Notable sites include the Church of San Martino and the Palazzo del Municipio, both of which contribute to the town's historical ambiance.

3. Lake Garda: The town's location on Lake Garda offers opportunities for water-based activities, such as boating, sailing, and swimming. The lake's scenic beauty provides a stunning backdrop for leisure activities, and lakeside promenades offer pleasant strolls with views of the water.

Activities and Attractions:
Visitors to Peschiera del Garda can enjoy a range of activities, including boat tours on Lake Garda, exploring the town's historic fortifications, and strolling through the charming streets of the historic centre. The town also hosts seasonal events and festivals, which add to its cultural vibrancy.

Amenities and Services:
Peschiera del Garda offers a variety of amenities, including restaurants, cafes, and shops. Visitors can sample local cuisine and purchase souvenirs from the town's shops. The town's waterfront area

provides opportunities for relaxation and outdoor dining, with scenic views of the lake.

Verona

Verona, located approximately 40 kilometres east of Mantua, is a city renowned for its rich history, architectural heritage, and cultural significance. Known as the setting for Shakespeare's famous play "Romeo and Juliet," Verona offers a wealth of historical and artistic attractions, making it a compelling destination for day trips.

Location and Accessibility:
Verona is situated in the Veneto region, and it is easily accessible from Mantua by car or train. The journey by car takes approximately 45 minutes, while regular train services connect Mantua to Verona, providing a convenient option for visitors. The city is well-connected by public transport and has a range of accommodation options for those wishing to extend their visit.

Historical and Cultural Significance:

Verona's history spans over two millennia, with influences from Roman, mediaeval, and Renaissance periods. The city's architectural and cultural landmarks reflect its diverse heritage.

1. The Arena of Verona: This ancient Roman amphitheatre is one of the best-preserved structures of its kind and continues to host performances and events. The Arena's impressive size and architectural features make it a must-see attraction.

2. Juliet's House: Associated with Shakespeare's play, Juliet's House is a popular tourist site, featuring a balcony that is said to be the inspiration for the famous scene in "Romeo and Juliet." The house includes a museum and offers insights into the story's enduring appeal.

3. Piazza delle Erbe: This historic square is the heart of Verona's old town and is surrounded by mediaeval buildings, including the Torre dei Lamberti and the Palazzo Maffei. The square also hosts a market, adding to its vibrant atmosphere.

4. Verona Cathedral: The Cathedral of Santa Maria Matricolare is a striking example of Romanesque

architecture, with a richly decorated interior and a beautiful cloister. The cathedral is an important religious and historical site in the city.

Activities and Attractions:
Visitors to Verona can explore the city's historic landmarks, enjoy guided tours that provide insights into its history and architecture, and experience local cuisine at traditional restaurants. Verona's vibrant cultural scene includes music, theatre, and festivals, offering a range of experiences for visitors.

Amenities and Services:
Verona provides a range of amenities, including dining options, shopping districts, and accommodation. The city's historic centre is pedestrian-friendly, making it easy to explore on foot. Information centres and guided tours are available to assist visitors in making the most of their time in Verona.

Local Vineyards and Farms

The region surrounding Mantua is known for its agricultural richness, including a variety of vineyards and farms that produce high-quality wines and local products. Exploring these local vineyards and farms offers an opportunity to experience the region's agricultural heritage and taste its distinctive flavours.

Location and Accessibility:
The vineyards and farms in the Mantua region are located in the countryside, with many situated in the provinces of Mantua and Verona. These agricultural sites are accessible by car from Mantua, with some farms and vineyards also offering guided tours and tastings. The scenic rural landscapes provide a picturesque setting for exploring local agriculture.

Local Vineyards:
1. Wine Production: The Mantua region is part of the larger wine-producing area of Lombardy, known for its quality wines. Local vineyards produce a range of red, white, and sparkling wines, including varieties such as Lambrusco and Pinot Grigio. Wine tours often include visits to vineyards, where visitors can learn about the winemaking process, from grape cultivation to fermentation and bottling.

2. Wine Tastings: Many vineyards offer wine tastings, allowing visitors to sample a selection of wines and experience the unique characteristics of the region's offerings. Tastings are often accompanied by explanations from knowledgeable staff, providing insights into the flavours and profiles of different wines.

Local Farms:
1. Agricultural Products: Local farms in the Mantua region produce a variety of agricultural products, including fresh fruits, vegetables, cheeses, and meats. Farm visits provide an opportunity to see traditional farming practices and sample local products.

2. Farm Tours: Guided tours of local farms offer insights into the production of regional products and the importance of sustainable agriculture. Visitors can explore fields, meet farmers, and learn about the techniques used in cultivating and harvesting crops.

Activities and Attractions:

Visitors to local vineyards and farms can enjoy wine tastings, farm tours, and seasonal festivals celebrating local produce. Many farms and vineyards offer educational programs and workshops, providing a deeper understanding of the region's agricultural practices and traditions.

Amenities and Services:
Local vineyards and farms often have on-site facilities, including tasting rooms, restaurants, and shops where visitors can purchase products. Many establishments also offer accommodations or partner with nearby hotels and B&Bs to provide convenient options for overnight stays.

The surrounding areas of Mantua offer a diverse range of day trip opportunities, from the Renaissance charm of Sabbioneta to the scenic beauty of Peschiera del Garda and the cultural richness of Verona. Local vineyards and farms add an agricultural dimension to the region's attractions, providing visitors with a taste of its culinary and viticultural heritage. Each destination offers unique experiences, contributing to the overall appeal of the Mantua region as a travel destination.

Chapter 7

Food and Dining

Traditional Mantuan Cuisine

Mantuan cuisine is a distinctive representation of the culinary traditions of the Lombardy region, reflecting the area's history, geography, and cultural influences. Known for its hearty and flavorful dishes, Mantuan cuisine combines local ingredients with traditional cooking methods to create a rich and varied gastronomic experience.

Key Ingredients and Dishes:

1. Pumpkin: A staple in Mantuan cuisine, pumpkin is used in various dishes, including tortelli di zucca, a traditional pasta stuffed with a pumpkin and amaretti filling. This dish is often served with a sage butter sauce or a sprinkle of grated Parmesan cheese.

2. Rice: Rice is a significant component of the local diet, particularly in dishes like risotto. Mantua is known for its risotto alla pilota, a flavorful dish made with rice, pork sausage, and a rich broth.

3. Cheese: Mantua produces a variety of cheeses, including Grana Padano and Mantova. These cheeses are used in cooking and served as part of antipasti platters.

4. Meats: The region's cuisine features a range of meat dishes, including brasato al vino rosso, a slow-cooked beef stew made with red wine, and salumi, such as pancetta and prosciutto.

5. Sweets: Desserts in Mantuan cuisine often feature local ingredients. Sbrisolona, a crumbly almond cake, and torta delle rose, a rose-shaped pastry, are popular traditional sweets.

Restaurants and Dining Locations:

1. Osteria dell'Oca: Located in Mantua's historic centre, this restaurant offers traditional Mantuan dishes in a cosy, rustic setting. Known for its tortelli di zucca and risotto alla pilota, it provides an

authentic dining experience. Address: Via delle Grazie, 5, 46100 Mantova. Phone: +39 0376 323 245. Cost per meal: €25-€40.

2. Ristorante La Ripa: This family-run restaurant specialises in regional cuisine, including various meat and pasta dishes. Address: Via della Ripa, 12, 46100 Mantova. Phone: +39 0376 322 430. Cost per meal: €30-€50.

3. Trattoria San Silvestro: Known for its traditional Mantuan flavours, Trattoria San Silvestro offers a range of local dishes in a casual, friendly environment. Address: Piazza San Silvestro, 2, 46100 Mantova. Phone: +39 0376 323 200. Cost per meal: €20-€35.

Websites:
- [Osteria dell'Oca](http://www.osteriadelloca.com)

Top Restaurants and Cafes

Mantua boasts a variety of dining establishments ranging from upscale restaurants to charming cafes, each offering a unique taste of local and international cuisine.

1. Antica Osteria Caffè dell'Angelo: A historic eatery offering a blend of Mantuan and Italian cuisine. The restaurant features a refined atmosphere and a menu that highlights local specialties alongside classic Italian dishes. Address: Via dell'Angelo, 3, 46100 Mantova. Phone: +39 0376 325 456. Cost per meal: €40-€70.

2. Il Cavallino Bianco: Located near Piazza Sordello, this restaurant offers a menu inspired by Mantuan traditions and contemporary cuisine. The stylish interior and innovative dishes make it a favourite for a special dining experience. Address: Via Giuseppe Mazzini, 8, 46100 Mantova. Phone: +39 0376 321 789. Cost per meal: €35-€60. Website: [Il Cavallino Bianco](http://www.cavallinobianco.com)

3. Caffè Centrale: A popular café in the heart of Mantua, Caffè Centrale is known for its selection of pastries, coffee, and light meals. It is an ideal spot for a casual breakfast or an afternoon coffee break. Address: Piazza delle Erbe, 10, 46100 Mantova.

Phone: +39 0376 324 567. Cost per meal: €10-€20.
Website: [Caffè
Centrale](http://www.caffecentrale.com)

4. Ristorante Il Bue e la Vacca: Renowned for its focus on high-quality meats and traditional Mantuan dishes, this restaurant offers a range of grilled and slow-cooked specialties in a refined setting. Address: Via dei Pini, 15, 46100 Mantova. Phone: +39 0376 326 789. Cost per meal: €40-€70.

Local Markets and Food Festivals

Mantua's markets and food festivals provide an excellent opportunity to experience local produce, traditional foods, and regional specialties. These events showcase the rich culinary heritage of the area and offer visitors a chance to sample and purchase a variety of goods.

1. Piazza delle Erbe Market: Held in the historic Piazza delle Erbe, this market is a vibrant hub for local produce, cheeses, meats, and artisanal products. The market operates weekly, offering a

diverse selection of fresh and seasonal items. Opening Hours: Tuesday to Saturday, 8:00 AM - 1:00 PM.

2. Mantova Gourmet Festival: This annual festival celebrates Mantuan cuisine and local products, featuring cooking demonstrations, tastings, and food-related events. Held in various locations throughout the city, the festival provides an immersive experience into local culinary traditions. Dates: Typically held in October.

3. Festa della Zucca: Dedicated to the pumpkin, a key ingredient in Mantuan cuisine, this festival takes place in Mantua and surrounding towns. It includes pumpkin-themed dishes, cooking contests, and local craft stalls. Dates: Late September to early October.

4. Mercato del Contadino: Held in various locations around Mantua, this farmers' market features organic produce, homemade cheeses, and traditional cured meats. The market emphasises sustainability and local farming practices. Opening Hours: Saturdays, 9:00 AM - 2:00 PM.

Cooking Classes and Food Tours

Cooking classes and food tours in Mantua offer an engaging way to learn about local cuisine, culinary techniques, and regional ingredients. These experiences provide hands-on learning opportunities and insights into the traditions of Mantuan cooking.

1. Mantova Cooking School: This school offers a range of cooking classes focusing on traditional Mantuan dishes, including pasta making, risotto preparation, and dessert crafting. Classes are led by experienced chefs and provide a comprehensive introduction to local cuisine. Address: Via Carlo d'Arco, 10, 46100 Mantova. Phone: +39 0376 321 456.

2. Food Tour Mantova: This guided tour takes participants through the city's historic centre, highlighting local markets, restaurants, and specialty food shops. The tour includes tastings of traditional dishes and insights into Mantuan culinary history. Tour Duration: Approximately 3 hours. Contact: +39 0376 322 789.

3. Gourmet Experiences Mantova: Offering private cooking classes and gourmet tours, this company provides personalised experiences tailored to individual interests and skill levels. Options include hands-on cooking classes, wine tastings, and visits to local farms. Contact: +39 0376 328 900.

4. Cooking with Nonna: This class focuses on traditional family recipes passed down through generations. Participants learn to prepare authentic Mantuan dishes in a warm, home-like setting. Address: Via delle Rose, 5, 46100 Mantova. Phone: +39 0376 322 345. Website: [Cooking with Nonna](http://www.cookingwithnonna.com)

Mantua's food and dining scene offers a rich tapestry of traditional cuisine, top-notch restaurants, local markets, and engaging culinary experiences. From savouring traditional dishes at local eateries to exploring vibrant markets and participating in cooking classes, visitors have numerous opportunities to immerse themselves in the region's gastronomic heritage. Whether you are a food enthusiast or simply looking to experience the local culture, Mantua provides a diverse and satisfying culinary journey.

Chapter 8

Accommodation

Luxury Hotels

Mantua offers a selection of luxury hotels that combine elegance, comfort, and high-end amenities to provide an exceptional stay. These hotels often feature exquisite architecture, gourmet dining options, and premium services, catering to both leisure and business travellers.

1. Hotel Casa Poli

Located in the heart of Mantua, Hotel Casa Poli provides a blend of historical charm and modern luxury. The hotel is housed in a historic building and features sophisticated decor, spacious rooms, and an array of amenities designed for a comfortable stay.

- Location: Via Ippolito Nievo, 16, 46100 Mantova

- Phone: +39 0376 322 710
- Cost per Night: Approximately €200-€300
-         Website: [Hotel   Casa
Poli](http://www.hotelcasapoli.com)

Features
- Gourmet restaurant offering a selection of local and international dishes
- Spa and wellness centre
- Fitness facilities
- Proximity to major attractions and historical sites

2. Hotel Mantova Palace

Hotel Mantova Palace is renowned for its luxurious accommodations and exceptional service. This modern hotel features contemporary design elements and provides a range of amenities to ensure a comfortable and memorable stay.

- Location: Viale delle Rimembranze, 16, 46100 Mantova
- Phone: +39 0376 321 200
- Cost per Night: Approximately €150-€250

Features:

- Spacious and well-appointed rooms
- On-site restaurant serving gourmet cuisine
- Business centre and conference facilities
- Wellness area with sauna and massage services

3. Palazzo Della Vittoria

Palazzo Della Vittoria offers a luxurious and historic ambiance, providing guests with an opulent experience in a beautifully restored building.

- Location: Piazza Della Vittoria, 1, 46100 Mantova
- Phone: +39 0376 326 100
- Cost per Night: Approximately €180-€300.

Features:
- Exquisite rooms and suites with classic decor
- Fine dining restaurant
- Fitness centre

Boutique Hotels and B&Bs

Boutique hotels and bed-and-breakfast establishments in Mantua offer a more personalised and intimate lodging experience. These accommodations are often characterised by unique design, individual charm, and exceptional hospitality.

1. Locanda Del Re Guerriero

 Situated in a central location, it provides a charming and personalised experience for guests.

- Location: Via dei Gonzaga, 12, 46100 Mantova
- Phone: +39 0376 323 456
- Cost per Night: Approximately €100-€150

Features:
- Cosy and elegantly decorated rooms
- Complimentary breakfast with local specialties
- Personalized service and attention to detail

2. B&B La Dolce Mantova

B&B La Dolce Mantova provides a comfortable and welcoming atmosphere in a residential area of the city. This bed-and-breakfast is known for its friendly hosts and homey environment.

- Location: Via Carlo d'Arco, 20, 46100 Mantova
- Phone: +39 0376 324 800
- Cost per Night: Approximately €80-€120

Features:
- Comfortable rooms with charming decor
- Homemade breakfast served daily
- Personalized service and local insights from the hosts
- Quiet and relaxing setting

3. Residenza Ariosto

Residenza Ariosto is a boutique guesthouse offering a refined and comfortable stay in Mantua. The property is known for its elegant decor and attentive service.

- Location: Via Ariosto, 5, 46100 Mantova
- Phone: +39 0376 326 700
- Cost per Night: Approximately €120-€180

Features:
- Stylish and comfortable rooms
- Convenient location near cultural landmarks
- Personalized guest services

Budget-Friendly Options

For travellers seeking more affordable accommodations, Mantua offers several budget-friendly options that provide good value without compromising comfort and quality.

1. Hotel Abacus

Hotel Abacus offers a practical and economical lodging option in Mantua. The hotel provides basic amenities and comfortable rooms at a reasonable price.

- Location: Via Ippolito Nievo, 14, 46100 Mantova
- Phone: +39 0376 323 900
- Cost per Night: Approximately €60-€100
-                      Website: [Hotel Abacus](http://www.hotelabacus.com)

Features:
- Simple and clean rooms
- Continental breakfast included

- Free Wi-Fi
- Central location with easy access to public transportation

2. B&B La Corte

B&B La Corte provides an affordable and cosy lodging option with a welcoming atmosphere. It is suitable for travellers looking for comfort on a budget.

- Location: Via della Corte, 8, 46100 Mantova
- Phone: +39 0376 322 500
- Cost per Night: Approximately €50-€80
- Website: [B&B La Corte](http://www.bblacorte.com)

Features:
- Comfortable rooms with essential amenities
- Homemade breakfast
- Friendly and attentive service
- Convenient location near the city centre

3. Ostello San Giovanni

Ostello San Giovanni is a hostel offering affordable accommodation options for budget-conscious travellers. It is ideal for those seeking basic amenities and a social atmosphere.

- Location: Via San Giovanni, 12, 46100 Mantova
- Phone: +39 0376 321 800
- Cost per Night: Approximately €30-€60

Features:
- Dormitory-style rooms and private rooms available
- Shared kitchen and lounge areas
- Basic amenities and services
- Friendly environment for meeting other travellers

Unique Stays (e.g., Historic Residences)

Mantua's unique stays include historic residences and properties with distinctive character, offering an immersive experience into the city's rich heritage.

1. Palazzo Gonzaga

Palazzo Gonzaga provides a unique lodging experience in a historic residence with ornate architecture and classic decor. The palatial atmosphere offers a glimpse into the grandeur of the Gonzaga family.

- Location: Via Gonzaga, 1, 46100 Mantova
- Phone: +39 0376 324 600
- Cost per Night: Approximately €250-€400
-                    Website: [Palazzo Gonzaga](http://www.palazzogonzaga.com)

Features:
- Luxurious rooms with historic furnishings
- Access to private gardens and courtyards
- Personalized service and historical insight.

2. Villa Minzi

Villa Minzi is a historic villa offering an elegant and serene environment. The villa's classic architecture and gardens provide a unique and memorable stay.

- Location: Via Minzi, 5, 46100 Mantova
- Phone: +39 0376 323 400
- Cost per Night: Approximately €200-€350

Features:
- Beautifully decorated rooms with period furnishings
- Expansive gardens and outdoor spaces
- Historical and cultural experiences
- Quiet location with scenic surroundings

3. Castello di San Giorgio Guesthouse

Castello di San Giorgio offers a distinctive stay in a historic castle, providing guests with a unique experience in a setting steeped in history. The guesthouse combines mediaeval charm with modern comforts.

- Location: Piazza Castello, 1, 46100 Mantova
- Phone: +39 0376 326 800
- Cost per Night: Approximately €150-€250
- Website: [Castello di San Giorgio Guesthouse](http://www.castellodisangiorgio.com)

Features:
- Rooms with historic and mediaeval decor
- Access to castle grounds and historical tours
- On-site dining options

Mantua offers a diverse range of accommodation options to suit different preferences and budgets. From luxurious hotels and boutique stays to budget-friendly lodgings and unique historic residences, visitors can find a suitable place to stay while exploring the rich cultural and historical heritage of this charming city.

Chapter 9

Practical Information

Travel Tips and Safety

When travelling to Mantua, it is essential to be aware of local travel tips and safety guidelines to ensure a smooth and enjoyable visit. The city, known for its rich history and beautiful architecture, is generally safe for tourists. However, adhering to some practical advice will enhance your experience.

General Safety Precautions

1. Personal Belongings: Keep a close eye on your personal belongings, especially in crowded areas such as markets and public transportation. Use a money belt or secure bag to safeguard valuables.

2. Emergency Services: In case of emergency, you can dial 112, which is the European Union

emergency number available for police, fire, and medical emergencies.

3. Travel Insurance: It is advisable to have travel insurance that covers medical emergencies, trip cancellations, and theft. Ensure your insurance policy covers you adequately during your stay.

4. Health Precautions: Mantua does not have specific health risks, but it is always wise to carry basic medications and be aware of any local health advisories. If you have specific medical conditions, ensure you have sufficient medication and know the location of the nearest pharmacy.

5. Local Laws: Familiarise yourself with local laws and regulations. For example, it is illegal to consume alcohol in public spaces and to smoke in enclosed public places.

Transportation Safety

1. Public Transport: Mantua has a well-organised public transportation system, including buses and trains. Be mindful of pickpockets and ensure your

tickets are validated as fines may apply if they are not.

2. Cycling: The city is bike-friendly, with dedicated cycling paths. However, be cautious of traffic and always use bike lanes where available.

3. Taxis and Ride-Sharing: Use licensed taxis or ride-sharing services for reliable transportation. Verify the taxi's credentials and agree on the fare before starting your journey.

Safety Around Historical Sites

1. Guided Tours: When exploring historical sites, consider joining a guided tour to gain insights and avoid getting lost. Guides can also help navigate any restricted areas or safety concerns.

2. Respect for Sites: Follow the rules and guidelines set by the site administrators. For instance, refrain from touching artefacts and adhere to designated pathways to preserve the integrity of the sites.

Emergency Contacts and Services

1. Local Police: Mantua's local police station can assist with various issues. The general contact number is +39 0376 322 111.

2. Hospitals: The main hospital in Mantua is Ospedale Carlo Poma. For emergencies, visit the emergency room or call +39 0376 327 000.

3. Pharmacies: Pharmacies are widespread throughout the city. In case of a medical emergency, the nearest pharmacy can be found by asking locals or using a mobile app.

Local Customs and Etiquette

Understanding local customs and etiquette enhances interactions and ensures respectful behaviour while visiting Mantua. Italians take pride in their culture and traditions, and adhering to these social norms demonstrates respect for the local way of life.

Greetings and Communication

1. Formal Greetings: When meeting someone for the first time, a handshake is the common form of greeting. In more formal settings, addressing individuals with their titles (such as Signore or Signora) followed by their last name is polite.

2. Personal Space: Italians value personal space and may stand close during conversations. However, it is important to be attentive to cues if someone seems uncomfortable with proximity.

3. Dining Etiquette: When dining, wait for everyone to be seated before starting your meal. It is polite to keep your hands on the table, but not your elbows. Additionally, it is customary to finish all food on your plate and to compliment the cook.

Dress Code

1. Casual Attire: In Mantua, casual attire is acceptable for most day-to-day activities. However, when visiting churches or formal establishments, modest clothing is recommended.

2. Dress for Dinner: For dinner, especially at higher-end restaurants, smart casual or formal attire

is preferred. Avoid wearing overly casual clothing such as shorts or flip-flops.

Social Norms

1. Tipping: Tipping is not obligatory but is appreciated. In restaurants, rounding up the bill or leaving a small amount (around 5-10%) is considered a courteous gesture. For taxis and other services, rounding up the fare is also common.

2. Respect for Culture: Show respect for local customs and traditions. For example, when visiting religious sites, dress conservatively and follow any guidelines regarding photography and behaviour.

3. Punctuality: Being punctual is valued in professional and social settings. Arriving on time for appointments and reservations is considered respectful.

Useful Phrases in Italian

Knowing a few key phrases in Italian can enhance your travel experience and facilitate smoother interactions with locals. While many people in Mantua speak English, especially in tourist areas, making an effort to speak the local language is appreciated.

Basic Greetings and Politeness

1. Buongiorno (bwohn-JOHR-noh) – Good morning
2. Buonasera (bwoh-nah-SEH-rah) – Good evening
3. Arrivederci (ahr-ree-veh-DEHR-chee) – Goodbye
4. Per favore (pehr fah-VOH-reh) – Please
5. Grazie (GRAHT-see-eh) – Thank you
6. Prego (PREH-go) – You're welcome

Common Questions

1. Dove si trova...? (DOH-veh see TROH-vah) – Where is...?
   - Example: Dove si trova il Museo di Palazzo Ducale? (Where is the Museo di Palazzo Ducale?)
2. Quanto costa? (KWAHN-toh KOH-stah) – How much does it cost?
3. Parla inglese? (PAHR-lah een-GLAY-zeh) – Do you speak English?

Dining and Shopping

1. Il conto, per favore (eel KON-toh pehr fah-VOH-reh) – The bill, please
2. Mi può consigliare un piatto tipico? (mee pwah kon-see-LYAH-reh oon PYAH-toh TEE-pee-koh) – Can you recommend a typical dish?
3. Dove posso trovare un supermercato? (DOH-veh POS-soh troh-VAH-reh oon soo-pehr-mehr-CAH-toh) – Where can I find a supermarket?

Emergency Situations

1. Ho bisogno di aiuto (oh bee-ZOH-nyoh dee ah-YOO-toh) – I need help
2. Dove si trova l'ospedale più vicino? (DOH-veh see TROH-vah loh-speh-DAH-leh pyoo vee-CHEE-noh) – Where is the nearest hospital?
3. Chiamate un'ambulanza (kee-ah-MAH-teh oon ahm-boo-LAHN-tsah) – Call an ambulance

Emergency Contacts and Services

In case of emergencies or unforeseen issues while in Mantua, knowing the appropriate contacts and services can provide peace of mind and assist in resolving situations efficiently.

Emergency Services

1. Police: The local police station handles various issues, including safety concerns and crime. Contact them at +39 0376 322 111 for non-emergencies or visit their station.

2. Medical Emergencies: Ospedale Carlo Poma provides comprehensive medical services. For emergencies, the emergency department can be reached at +39 0376 327 000.

3. Fire Department: The fire department is available for fire-related emergencies and can be contacted by dialling 115.

Useful Contacts

1. Tourist Information: The Mantua Tourist Information Office provides assistance with travel information, maps, and local recommendations. Located at Piazza Martiri di Belfiore, 1, you can contact them at +39 0376 368 500.

2. Pharmacies: For pharmaceutical needs, there are several pharmacies throughout the city. The main pharmacy, Farmacia Comunale, is located at Via Pietro da Castelbelbo, 5, and can be reached at +39 0376 322 777.

3. Embassy Contacts: If you require consular assistance, contact your country's embassy or consulate. The Italian Ministry of Foreign Affairs website provides contact details for various embassies.

Additional Resources

1. Local Transportation Information: For public transportation details, including bus and train schedules, visit the local transportation authority's website or contact them at +39 0376 321 111.

2. Local Services Directory: The Mantua city directory provides contact information for various local services, including utility companies and community organisations. Visit the city's official website for access to the directory.

By adhering to safety guidelines, respecting local etiquette, and knowing essential contacts, you can fully appreciate the rich cultural and historical offerings of this captivating city.

Conclusion

As you conclude this journey through the vibrant city of Mantua, it becomes evident why this gem of Lombardy deserves a spot on your travel itinerary. Nestled in the heart of northern Italy, Mantua offers a unique blend of history, culture, and natural beauty that captivates visitors and leaves lasting impressions.

From its Renaissance splendour under the Gonzaga dynasty to its contemporary charm, Mantua stands as a testament to Italy's rich cultural heritage. The city's architectural marvels, such as the Ducal Palace and Palazzo del Te, reveal the grandeur of past eras and the artistic brilliance of figures like Andrea Mantegna and Giulio Romano. Each structure, meticulously preserved and celebrated, tells a story of the city's illustrious past and its significant role in European history.

Walking through Mantua's streets, one encounters a harmonious blend of historical and modern life. The city centre, with its vibrant piazzas and majestic buildings, provides a picturesque setting for leisurely exploration. Piazza Sordello, the Ducal Palace, and the Mantua Cathedral offer a glimpse into the city's rich architectural legacy, while the Church of San Andrea and Rotonda di San Lorenzo provide a deeper connection to Mantua's spiritual and artistic traditions.

For those keen on immersing themselves in the local culture, the museums and art galleries present a treasure trove of artistic and historical artefacts. The Museo di Palazzo Ducale and Museo di Palazzo Te stand out for their extensive collections and their role in preserving the city's artistic heritage. Meanwhile, the Accademia Virgiliana and the State Archives offer insights into the intellectual and cultural pursuits that have shaped Mantua over the centuries.

Outdoor enthusiasts will find ample opportunities to engage with Mantua's natural beauty. The Parco del Mincio and the Mincio Cycle Path offer serene settings for relaxation and recreation, while boat tours on the Mincio River provide a unique perspective of the city's landscape. These outdoor activities allow visitors to appreciate Mantua not just as a historical destination but as a place where nature and culture coexist in harmony.

The city's culinary scene is another highlight, with traditional Mantuan cuisine offering a delightful array of flavours. From rich risottos to delectable tortelli di zucca, dining in Mantua is an experience to be savoured. Top restaurants, local markets, and food festivals showcase the region's gastronomic diversity, while cooking classes and food tours provide a hands-on approach to exploring Mantuan culinary traditions.

When it comes to accommodation, Mantua caters to a range of preferences and budgets. Whether you seek the opulence of luxury hotels, the charm of boutique accommodations, or the affordability of budget-friendly options, the city offers a variety of choices. Unique stays, including historic residences, add an extra layer of charm to your visit, allowing you to experience Mantua from a distinctive perspective.

In your exploration of Mantua, practical information such as travel tips, local customs, and useful phrases will enhance your experience. Understanding local etiquette and being prepared for emergencies ensures a smooth and enjoyable visit, allowing you to fully engage with all that this remarkable city has to offer.

In essence, Mantua is more than just a destination; it is an experience that enriches the soul. Its rich history, architectural wonders, vibrant culture, and picturesque landscapes make it a must-visit location for travellers seeking to delve into Italy's heritage while enjoying modern comforts.

We encourage you to immerse yourself in the beauty and charm of Mantua. Explore its historical sites, savour its culinary delights, and embrace the warmth of its local culture. Whether you are drawn by its Renaissance art, its outdoor activities, or its culinary offerings, Mantua promises to leave a lasting impression on your heart and mind. As you plan your visit, let the allure of Mantua guide you to this enchanting city, where history and culture come to life in the most captivating ways.

.

Made in the USA
Las Vegas, NV
06 February 2025

17649103R00075